Kit's Friendship Fun

American Girl®

Table of Contents

If you've read the stories about Kit, you know that life for girls growing up in the 1930s was different than it is for girls today. But some things about growing up haven't changed at all. Girls still love playing games, making crafts, and cooking treats with their friends. In fact, having fun with friends is still one of the best parts of being a girl, just as it was for Kit and Ruthie.

Learning about the crafts, meals, and games of the 1930s will help you understand what it was like to grow up the way Kit did. Enjoying these activities of the past will bring history to life for you and your friends.

Tips for You

 *The most important tip is to **work with an adult**. When you see this symbol, it means you will need an adult's help with that step.*

- *Read all the directions before you start.*

- *Wash your hands with soap before and after your project. Wear an apron, tie back your hair, and roll up your sleeves.*

- *Don't use the stove or oven without an adult's supervision. Turn off the stove burners or oven as soon as you are done.*

- *Be careful with sharp knives and scissors.*

- *Put covers back on containers tightly. If you spill, clean up right away.*

- *Leave your work area as clean as you found it. Wash dishes, put away supplies, and throw away garbage.*

Cooking Tips

1 Get an adult's help when the directions tell you to, or if you're not sure what to do. Have an adult help you use cooking equipment properly.

2 Before you start to cook, gather everything you will need. Set the ingredients and utensils where you can reach them easily.

3 When you stir or mix, hold the bowl or pan steady on a flat surface, not in your arms.

4 Use potholders when touching hot pans, to protect yourself from burns. Protect countertops by using trivets under hot pots and pans.

5 Keep hot foods hot and cold foods cold. If you plan to make things early and serve them later, store them properly. Foods that could spoil belong in the refrigerator. Wrap foods well.

Craft Tips

1.  Get an adult's help when the directions tell you to, or if you're not sure what to do. Have an adult help you use tools properly.

2. You can find most of the materials listed in this book in your home or at craft and fabric stores. If an item is starred (*), look at the bottom of the materials list to read more about it or find out where you can get it. Gather all your supplies before you start.

3. Select a good work area for your craft projects. Pick a place that has plenty of light and is out of reach of pets and little brothers and sisters.

4. Ask your friends to bring aprons or smocks. Have everyone tie back her hair and roll up her sleeves. Cover the work area with newspapers.

5. If there's a step that doesn't make sense to you, try it out with a piece of scrap paper or fabric first. Practicing often helps.

6. If your crafts don't turn out exactly like the pictures in the book, that's perfectly all right! The pictures are just there to give you ideas. Crafts become more meaningful when you add your own personal touch.

Sewing Tips

Threading the Needle
Wet one end of the thread in your mouth. Push the thread through the eye of the needle.

Pull about 5 inches of thread through the needle. Then tie a double knot near the end of the long tail of thread.

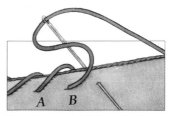

Sewing a Backstitch
Bring the needle up at A. Go down at B. Come up at C and go down at A. Come up at D and go down at C. Keep going!

Sewing a Whipstitch
Bring the needle up at A. Pull the thread over the edge of the fabric, and come up at B. Keep going!

Kit's Life and Times

Kit's mornings got off to a fast start. Even on school days, she had to collect the laundry and dust the upstairs hallway. To make the chores more fun, Kit invented a few tricks: she put on Dad's dirty socks over her shoes and skated down the hallway to dust the floor. Then she slid down the banister, polishing it as she went! After that, she helped Mother make breakfast for the boarders.

During the Depression, many families took in *boarders,* or paying guests, as a way to earn some money. When Kit's father lost his job, Mother decided to take in boarders so that the Kittredges could still make their monthly *mortgage payment*, the money they owed the bank for their house. For people who didn't own homes or who had lost their homes in the Depression, boarding with a family was less expensive than renting an apartment.

*This boarding house also served inexpensive meals for **drop-ins**, people who weren't boarders but needed a hot meal.*

When Stirling, Mrs. Howard, and the other boarders first moved in, Kit resented all the extra chores she had to do each day, and she wished the boarders would move out. Then she saw that without the rent money the boarders paid, her family might lose their house. Although it wasn't always easy for so many people to live together in one house, Kit realized how important it was to keep the boarders happy and provide a nice place for them to live. The Kittredges and their boarders needed each other, and everyone worked hard to get along.

The Depression affected children like Kit in other ways, too. Girls who had been best friends for years often found their situations dramatically changed with little warning. A friend might suddenly have to move away, with barely enough time to say good-bye. And there were awkward moments when one friend's family still had enough money to afford luxuries like movies and new clothes while

In the 1930s, girls enjoyed simple pleasures like climbing trees and sharing favorite books.

another friend's family was struggling to make ends meet. These challenges were a real test of friendship. Good friends like Kit and Ruthie had to set aside feelings of pride and shame, and focus on the important things that didn't require money—loyalty, friendship, and having fun together.

Kit's Aunt Millie proved that you don't need a lot of money to have a good time. All you need is a lively imagination, a dash of ingenuity, and—most important of all—a positive attitude.

When they moved, many families took along only what they could fit into the back of a pickup truck.

As many people discovered in the 1930s, growing vegetables and raising chickens was hard work, but it was fun, too. And having a new outfit was nicer than wearing hand-me-downs, even if the outfit was made from an old feed sack!

Chickens were easy and cheap to raise, so families often sold eggs during the Depression, just like the Kittredges.

Kit, Stirling, and Ruthie were fascinated with Aunt Millie's creative ways of getting food, making clothing, and even throwing a party. When the time came for Kit's birthday party, everyone pitched in, including the boarders, and Kit's friends agreed that the Penny-Pincher Party was the best birthday party anyone had ever had.

Today, many grandparents and older people who lived through the Depression look back on it as one of the best times to grow up. Even though times were hard and people sometimes went hungry, what they remember today is the way everyone—family, neighbors, and friends—pulled together to help one another. Girls like Kit discovered that friendship and shared fun can get you through even the toughest times—and leave the best memories.

Animal feed came in cloth sacks with bright, colorful patterns. Many girls happily wore feed-sack fashions!

9

Boarding House Breakfast

Every morning Kit helped Mother get breakfast ready. Most days they served oatmeal, because it was cheap and filling. Mother made it special by adding a peach slice to each serving. When they had extra fruit, they made treats like ambrosia or banana fritters. After Aunt Millie brought the chickens, Mother often made goldenrod eggs. On holidays, Mother brought the waffle iron right to the table, set it on a trivet, and made waffles for everyone.

After breakfast, Kit and Aunt Millie did the family's mending. Kit paid close attention to Aunt Millie's clever tricks for getting more wear out of old clothes and sheets, so that she could add something new to the *Waste Not, Want Not Almanac*.

Oatmeal with Peaches

Sprinkle on a little sugar and stir in some cream or milk for a wholesome breakfast.

Ingredients

- 3½ cups water
- ¼ teaspoon salt
- 2 cups old-fashioned rolled oats
- Sliced peaches, fresh or canned

Equipment

- Measuring cups and spoons
- Saucepan
- Wooden spoon
- Potholder
- Bowls

Serves 4–6

1 Measure the water into the saucepan. Add the salt.

2 Place the saucepan on medium heat. Heat the water until it *boils*, or bubbles rapidly.

3 Stir in the oatmeal. Cook the oatmeal for 5 minutes, stirring occasionally.

4 Have an adult help you remove the oatmeal from the stove.

5 Spoon the oatmeal into bowls. Place a few peach slices on top and serve hot.

Step 3

Ambrosia

*This simple fruit salad makes
a healthy dessert, too.*

Ingredients

- 3 medium-sized
  seedless oranges
- 6 tablespoons
  powdered sugar
- ½ cup shredded
  coconut

Equipment

- Sharp paring knife
- Serving dish
- Measuring cups
  and spoons

Serves 4–6

1  Have an adult help you use the
paring knife to peel the rinds off the
oranges. Carefully remove the white
inner peel from the oranges, too.

2 Cut each peeled orange along the
membranes, then lift out each section,
leaving the membranes behind.

Step 2

3 Line the bottom of the serving dish
with orange sections. Sprinkle on some
of the powdered sugar and coconut.
Continue layering fruit, sugar, and
coconut until the dish is filled.

4 Chill the ambrosia until you are ready
to serve it.

Goldenrod Eggs

With the chickens from Aunt Millie, Kit's family had plenty of eggs. This recipe was elegant enough to serve for supper.

Ingredients

- 6 hard-boiled eggs, peeled
- 4 tablespoons butter
- ½ cup flour
- Salt
- Pepper
- 2 cups milk
- 6 pieces of bread
- Chopped parsley

Equipment

- Sharp knife
- Cutting board
- Spoon
- Sieve
- Mixing bowl
- Measuring cups and spoons
- 2 saucepans
- Wooden spoon
- Toaster

Serves 6

1 Slice the eggs in half lengthwise. Scoop out the yolks and put them in the sieve.

2 Place the sieve with the yolks over the bowl. Use the spoon to mash the yolks through the sieve. Set the bowl aside.

Step 2

3 Have an adult help you coarsely chop the egg whites. Set them aside.

4 Melt the butter in a saucepan over low heat. Be careful not to let it burn.

5 Stir the flour, salt, and pepper into the melted butter. Stir the mixture constantly until it thickens. Take the saucepan off the burner.

Step 5

6   In the other saucepan, heat the milk on medium-high, stirring constantly, until it's hot.

7   Slowly add the hot milk to the flour-and-butter mixture. Stir the mixture well. When all of the milk has been added, put the flour mixture back on the burner set at medium-high.

Step 7

8   Bring the sauce to a boil, stirring constantly until it thickens. Turn the burner to low.

9   Cook the sauce for 3 more minutes. Remove the sauce from the heat.

10 Add the chopped egg whites and half of the egg yolks to the sauce.

11 Toast the bread. Set each piece on a plate. Spoon the sauce over the toast. Then spoon the remaining egg yolk over the sauce. Add chopped parsley for a final touch.

Step 11

How to Hard-Boil Eggs

Put the eggs into a pan and cover them with water. Heat the water until it bubbles rapidly. Then turn off the heat and cover the pan. After 15 minutes, have an adult help you run cold water over the eggs. Then peel them, or place them in the refrigerator overnight and peel them the next day.

Waffles

Waffles make any breakfast festive and fun. In Kit's day, waffles were sometimes served with fruit syrup—yum!

Ingredients

- 1⅔ cups flour
- ⅓ cup yellow cornmeal
- 4 tablespoons baking powder
- ½ teaspoon salt
- ⅓ cup rolled oats*
- 2 cups milk
- 1 tablespoon honey
- 1 teaspoon vanilla
- 3 eggs
- ⅓ cup oil
- Butter
- Syrup

Equipment

- Sifter
- Large mixing bowl
- Measuring cups and spoons
- Medium mixing bowl
- 2 small bowls
- Wooden spoon
- Electric mixer
- Waffle iron

*Quick oats or old-fashioned

Serves 6–8

1 Put the sifter into the large mixing bowl. Measure the flour, cornmeal, baking powder, and salt into the sifter. Sift them into the bowl. Add the oats, then set the bowl aside.

2 Measure the milk, honey, and vanilla into the medium mixing bowl. Set the bowl aside.

3 Have an adult help you separate the egg whites and the egg yolks, as shown. Let the whites drop into one small bowl. Drop the yolks into the other small bowl.

16

   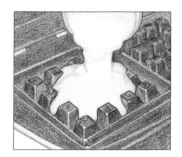

4 Stir the egg yolks into the milk mixture. Slowly stir the milk mixture into the dry ingredients. Stir in the oil.

5 Have an adult help you beat the egg whites with the mixer until the whites are shiny and slightly stiff, with the whites forming soft peaks when you pull out the beaters.

6 *Fold,* or gently mix, the egg whites into the waffle batter. The batter will be fluffy, with some lumps of egg white.

7 To cook the waffles, have an adult help you follow the directions for your waffle iron. Serve the waffles warm with butter and syrup.

Banana Fritters

Try this tasty breakfast treat for a change of pace.

Ingredients

- 6 bananas
- ½ cup powdered sugar
- ¼ cup lemon juice

Batter:
- Vegetable oil for deep-frying
- 1½ cups flour
- ¼ teaspoon salt
- 2 teaspoons baking powder
- 1 egg
- 1 cup milk

Topping:
- 2 tablespoons powdered sugar

Equipment

- Sharp knife
- Cutting board
- 2 mixing bowls
- Measuring cups and spoons
- Deep-fat fryer or deep, heavy skillet or pan
- Cooking thermometer
- Paper towels
- Electric mixer
- Rubber spatula
- Tablespoon
- Slotted spoon
- Sieve or sifter

Serves 4-6

1 Peel the bananas. Cut each banana into four sections, then cut each section in half lengthwise.

2 Place the bananas in a mixing bowl. Sprinkle them with powdered sugar. Add the lemon juice, and let stand for 30 minutes.

Step 1

3 Pour the oil into the fryer or skillet. The oil should be about 1½ inches deep. Clip the thermometer to the edge of the pan. The tip of the thermometer should be in the oil, but not touching the bottom or sides of the pan. Lay a pile of paper towels on the counter.

Step 3

4 Measure the flour, salt, and baking powder into the other mixing bowl.

5 Add the egg and the milk. Have an adult help you use the electric mixer to beat the mixture until it is thick. Turn off the mixer and scrape the sides of the bowl with the rubber spatula.

6 Place a few bananas in the fritter batter and turn them until they are covered.

Step 6

7 Heat the oil to 350°. Have an adult use the tablespoon to gently slip a batter-covered banana into the oil. Fry it for about 1 minute, then use the slotted spoon to turn the fritter. Fry another minute, or until it is golden brown.

Step 7

8 Have an adult remove the fritter from the oil and place it on the paper towels.

9 Repeat steps 6 through 8 until all of the fritters have been cooked.

Step 8

10 Measure 2 tablespoons of powdered sugar into a sieve or sifter. Dust the fritters with a fine layer of sugar. Serve immediately.

The Perfect Fruit

Bananas were popular during the Depression. They were cheap, nutritious, and needed no refrigeration. Because bananas were imported year-round, they could be sold on the street when apples were out of season.

Mosaic Tile Trivet

*Protect the table
by resting hot pots on
this sturdy trivet.*

Materials

- 2 foam paintbrushes,
  1 inch wide
- Acrylic paints
- Craft board,
  6¾ by 6¾ inches
- 7 jumbo craft sticks
- Glue
- Stained glass pieces*
- Measuring spoon
- White tile grout
- Water
- Plastic bowl
- Rubber spatula
- Sponge, slightly
  dampened

 *Available at craft stores.
Or make your own: Place
old tiles or old china plates
between folded newspapers,
and hit gently with a
hammer. Wear goggles to
protect your eyes.*

1 Use the foam paintbrushes to paint the
craft board and 6 craft sticks. Let the
paint dry for 15 minutes. Add a second
coat of paint if needed.

2 Glue one craft stick on each side of the
craft board. Then glue a craft stick on
the top and on the bottom. The ends
will overlap, as shown.

Step 2

3 Place the glass pieces on the craft
board and make a design. Then glue
the pieces in place. Handle the glass
carefully—the edges are very sharp.

Step 3

4 Use the extra glass pieces to fill in the
empty areas of the board. Glue them
in place.

20

5 While the glue is drying, mix the grout. Add 3 tablespoons of grout and 1 tablespoon of water to the plastic bowl. Mix them with the unpainted craft stick. The grout should have a thick, smooth consistency, similar to creamy peanut butter. Add more grout or water as needed.

Step 6

6 Use the spatula to spread the grout over the glass pieces. Make sure to fill all of the spaces between the glass pieces.

7 Let the grout dry for 15 minutes. Then wipe the grout off the top of the glass pieces gently with the damp sponge. Rinse and wring out the sponge. Keep wiping until all of the excess grout is removed. Let the grout sit overnight.

8 Glue the last 2 painted craft sticks onto each side of the craft board. Let dry. Now you can set a hot dish on the trivet at your next family meal!

Sew a Patch

Got a hole in a favorite shirt or pair of pants? Don't despair. Do what Kit would have done— patch it up!

  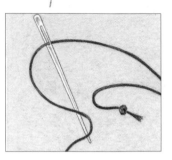

Materials

- Scissors
- Fabric of your choice
- Straight pins
- Iron and ironing board
- Piece of clothing with a hole or stain
- Thread
- Medium sewing needle

1 Cut a piece of fabric big enough to cover the area you wish to patch.

2 Fold under the raw edges of the patch, about ½ inch from the edge. Have an adult help you iron the patch flat. Pin the patch to the clothing to cover the hole or stain.

3 Cut an 18-inch piece of thread. Thread the needle, and tie a knot at the other end of the thread.

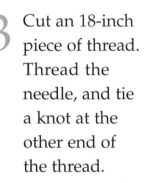

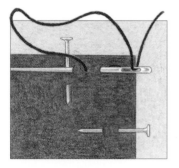 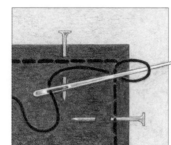

4 Use the back-stitch shown on page 5 to sew the patch onto your clothing.

5 When you're finished, tie a knot close to your last stitch and cut off the extra thread.

Thrifty Crafts

In the 1930s, most people could not afford new clothes or new things for their homes. If they needed something, they had to make it themselves out of whatever materials were available. Worn clothing could be cut down to fit a smaller child. Moth-eaten sweaters could be unraveled and re-knitted into hats and mittens. Even rags could be made into quilts or rugs. The eighth-graders below are braiding corn husks to make mats—a thrifty use for materials that most farms had plenty of.

In the Backyard

Before the Depression, Kit's backyard was a showcase for Mother's flower beds and garden parties. After Dad lost his job, things changed. Kit's mother had no time for flower gardening. And once Aunt Millie brought chickens and put in a vegetable garden, the yard looked— and sounded—more like a farm!

Still, that didn't stop Aunt Millie from throwing a wonderful back-yard party for Kit's birthday. There was still enough lawn for games, and Aunt Millie even showed Kit's friends how to pick tender dandelion leaves to make a free salad.

Kit also enjoyed picking juicy tomatoes for sandwiches and straw-berries for jam. In fact, Kit found that she liked the new, useful backyard even better than the old, elegant one.

Sun Print Greeting Card

Watching misty shapes form on the light-sensitive paper is half the fun of this card craft!

Materials

- Piece of glass, 5 by 7 inches
- Glass baking dish, at least 6 by 8 inches
- 2 cups warm water
- ¼ cup fixer crystals*
- Wooden spoon
- Photographic paper, 5 by 7 inches*
- Piece of cardboard, 5 by 7 inches
- Ferns, dried flowers, or whatever you would like to print
- Pair of rubber gloves
- Rubber spatula
- Colored construction paper, 8 by 11 inches
- Glue stick

* Available at camera shops

1 Clean the glass and the baking dish with dish soap and water, and dry them.

2 Pour 2 cups of warm water in the dish. Carefully add ¼ cup of fixer crystals to the water. Use the wooden spoon to stir the mixture. Set mixture aside.

3 Take one sheet of photographic paper out of its envelope and lay it on the cardboard, shiny side up.

4 Arrange the items you are printing on the paper. Place the glass over the paper and the items. Handle the glass carefully.

Step 4

5 Put the cardboard with the paper, items, and glass outdoors in bright sunlight for 100 seconds. The paper will turn a grayish purple. Bring everything inside.

6 Carefully remove the glass and the items. Put on the rubber gloves and place the paper in the fixer solution. Stir the fixer around and over the print for 2 minutes. Try not to touch the surface of the print. If the print starts to fade, take it out of the fixer sooner.

7 Rinse the print under cool running water for 6 minutes. Let the print drip dry, then lay it on a flat surface.

8 Use the rubber spatula to scrape the last water droplets off the print. The print will change color as it dries.

Step 8

9 Fold the piece of construction paper in half to make a card. Use the glue stick to glue the print onto the front of the card.

Staying in Touch

In Kit's time, telephones were a luxury, so most people kept in touch by mail. Cards were as popular then as they are today. Girls who couldn't afford store-bought cards simply made their own.

27

Scrapbook

Fill this handsome homemade scrapbook with photos of your friends, or use it as a journal.

Materials

- 8 sheets of paper, 11 by 17 inches
- Ruler
- Pencil
- Manila folder
- Scissors
- 2 large paper clips
- Darning needle
- Thread
- Ribbon, 1½ inches wide, 14¼ inches long
- 2 pieces of heavy cardboard, 8¾ by 11¼ inches
- Craft glue
- 2 sheets wrapping paper, 10¾ by 15¼ inches
- Rolling pin
- 2 sheets colored paper, 11 by 17 inches

1 Fold each sheet of paper in half, separately. Stack the pages inside each other to make the pages of your book.

Step 1

2 Measure 2 inches from the fold of the folder. Draw a line across the folder at the 2-inch mark. Cut along the line through both layers of the folder, to make a 2-inch-wide, folded strip.

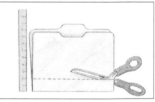
Step 2

3 Trim the top and bottom of the folded strip at an angle, as shown. Place the pages inside the strip.

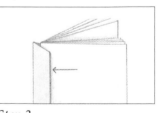
Step 3

4 Open the book and lay it flat. Clip the pages and the strip together with paper clips. The strip forms the book's spine.

5 Using the ruler and pencil, make marks down the center crease at 1½, 3½, 5½, 7½, and 9½ inches from the top.

Steps 4 and 5

6 Carefully poke a hole through each pencil mark with the darning needle.

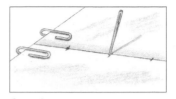

Step 6

7 Cut a 24-inch piece of thread, and thread the needle. Push the needle in at A, starting from the outside of the spine. Come out at B. Go in at C, and come back out at B. Go in at D, and come out at E. Go back in at D. Come out at A.

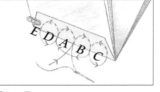

Step 7

8 The loose ends of thread should be on the outside of the spine. Tie them in a double knot, and trim the ends.

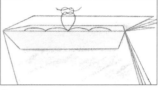

Step 8

9 To make the book cover, lay the ribbon flat. Glue a piece of cardboard on each side of the ribbon. Be sure to leave 1½ inches of ribbon at the top and the bottom, and ½ inch in the middle.

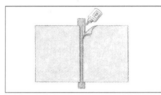

Step 9

10 Glue the wrapping paper to the cardboard covers, overlapping the ribbon edges slightly. Leave 2 inches at the top and bottom, and 2 inches at the sides. Roll out any air bubbles. Trim off the corners of the paper diagonally.

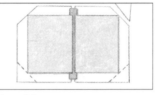

Step 10

11 Fold the top, bottom, and sides of the paper over the cardboard. Glue down.

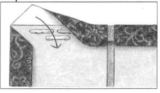

Step 11

12 Glue the strip of manila folder, which you stitched to the pages in step 7, to the inside of the front and back covers.

Step 12

13 Glue the 2 sheets of colored paper between the covers and the pages, to form the endpapers. Once the glue dries, your scrapbook is ready for use!

Step 13

Clutch Purse

This pretty purse is the perfect size for hair bands and barrettes. Its cheery flower design makes it just right for a garden party!

Materials

- Piece of felt, 9 by 12 inches
- Ruler
- Straight pins
- Embroidery floss
- Scissors
- Needle
- Thread, the same color as the felt
- Sew-on snap, size no. 3
- Pencil
- Sheet of tracing paper
- Scraps of felt
- Fabric glue

1 Hold the felt so that the top and bottom are 9 inches and the sides are 12 inches. Fold the bottom up 4 inches. Pin the sides together above the fold.

Step 1

2 Cut an 18-inch piece of floss. The floss is made up of 6 strands. Separate 2 strands.

3 Thread the needle with 2 strands. Tie a double knot at the other end of the floss.

4 Use the whipstitch from page 5 to sew the sides of the purse together. When you've finished, tie a knot close to your last stitch and cut off the extra floss. Take out the pins.

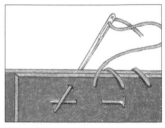

Step 4

5 To sew on the snap, cut a 12-inch piece of thread and thread the needle. Tie a double knot at the end of the thread.

6 Sew the half of the snap with the knob to the back of the flap. Center it ½ inch from the edge of the flap. Sew in and out of the holes, as shown, to secure the snap tightly to the felt.

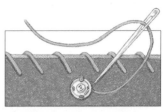
Step 6

7 Sew the other half of the snap to the front of the purse. Be sure it is aligned with the first snap so that the purse will snap closed.

Step 7

8 Use the pencil to trace the flower and leaf patterns shown on page 90 onto tracing paper. Cut out the patterns.

9 Pin the patterns to the felt scraps. Cut out the flower and leaves from the felt, and unpin the patterns.

Step 10

10 Glue the flower and leaves onto the front flap of the purse, and let it dry.

All Dressed Up

When girls went out in public in the 1930s, they usually dressed up with a hat and purse. These well-dressed children are waiting in line at a movie theater.

Fruity Freezer Jam

This easy jam needs no cooking at all! It's great in sandwiches and delicious over vanilla ice cream.

Ingredients

- 20 ounces fresh strawberries
- 4 cups sugar
- 2 tablespoons fresh lemon juice
- 1 pouch liquid pectin

Equipment

- Paring knife
- Cutting board
- Large mixing bowl
- Potato masher
- Measuring cups and spoons
- Wooden spoon
- Small mixing bowl
- Jars or plastic containers with lids

1 Use the paring knife to remove the stems from the strawberries. Cut the strawberries in half and put them in the large mixing bowl.

2 Use the potato masher to crush the berries. Measure 2 cups of crushed berries. (If there's extra, set it aside— don't use it in the jam.)

3 Stir the 4 cups of sugar into the 2 cups of berries. Mix well, then let stand for 10 minutes.

Sweet Harvest

People often used fruit that was too bruised to be sold in stores for making jam and juice. The fruit cost very little, and it tasted just as good! This family is running an apple press to make apple cider.

4 Measure the lemon juice into the small bowl. Add the liquid pectin and stir well.

5 Add the pectin mixture to the strawberries. Stir well for 3 minutes, until the sugar is completely dissolved.

6 Pour the jam into jars. If you plan to freeze the jam, use plastic containers, and leave a ½-inch space at the top of each container.

7 Cover the jars or containers. Let them sit at room temperature overnight, or until the jam has set. Store the jam for up to 3 weeks in the refrigerator, or freeze it for up to 1 year.

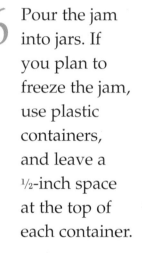

Club Sandwiches

The club is a double-decker sandwich with lettuce, tomato, and meat. Kit's mother might have served these fancy sandwiches at her garden club parties!

Ingredients

- 8 slices bacon
- 2 tomatoes
- 12 slices bread
- Mayonnaise
- Lettuce
- Cooked chicken breast, sliced

Equipment

- Paper towels
- Skillet
- Tongs
- Sharp knife
- Cutting board
- Toaster
- Knife
- 16 toothpicks

Serves 4

1 Place 2 layers of paper towels on the counter next to the stove. Separate the bacon strips and place them side by side in the skillet.

2 Turn the heat to medium-high. Have an adult help you cook the bacon until the edges start to curl. Use the tongs to turn over the bacon slices. Continue cooking, turning the bacon frequently.

3 When the bacon is golden brown and crisp, lift it out of the skillet and put it on the paper towels to cool and drain.

4 Have an adult help you thinly slice the tomatoes.

Step 2

Step 3

5 Toast the bread. For each sandwich, you will need 3 pieces of toast.

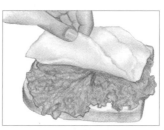

Step 6

6 Spread mayonnaise on 1 piece of toast. Arrange the lettuce and chicken.

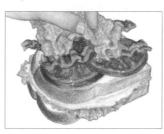

Step 7

7 Place another piece of toast on top. Spread mayonnaise on it, then arrange the tomato slices, bacon, and lettuce.

8 Cover the sandwich with another piece of toast. Have an adult help you cut the sandwich into triangles. Insert a toothpick through each triangle.

9 Repeat steps 6 through 8 for each sandwich. Serve immediately.

Garden Fresh

Picking tomatoes was tiring work, but eating them was a pleasure. Fresh off the vine and warmed by the sun, homegrown tomatoes tasted far better than store-bought.

Apple Kuchen

Kuchen means "cake" in German. Your whole kitchen will smell delicious while this cake is baking!

Ingredients

Kuchen:
- Butter to grease baking pan
- 2½ cups flour
- 2 teaspoons baking powder
- ½ teaspoon salt
- ½ cup butter
- ½ cup sugar
- 2 eggs
- ½ cup milk
- 2 teaspoons vanilla

Apple Topping:
- 5 medium apples
- ½ cup butter
- ½ cup sugar
- 2 teaspoons cinnamon
- ⅔ cup apple jelly
- Whipped cream

Equipment

- Baking pan, 9 by 13 inches
- Sifter
- 3 large mixing bowls
- Measuring cups and spoons
- Electric mixer
- Rubber spatula
- Vegetable peeler
- Sharp knife
- Cutting board
- Small saucepan
- Wooden spoon
- Toothpick
- Potholders
- Pastry brush

1 Preheat the oven to 375°. Grease the baking pan with butter. Set it aside.

2 Put the sifter into a mixing bowl. Measure the flour, baking powder, and salt into the sifter, then sift them into the bowl. Set aside.

Step 2

3 Put the butter in another mixing bowl. Add the sugar. With an adult's help, use the electric mixer to beat the mixture until it is creamy.

4 Crack the eggs into the butter mixture. Beat well. Then gradually add the dry ingredients, beating with the mixer.

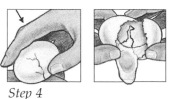

Step 4

5 Add the milk and vanilla. Beat the batter until it is smooth.

6 Use the rubber spatula to spread the batter into the baking pan.

Step 6

7 🖐 To make the apple topping, peel and core the apples. Have an adult help you slice them very thin.

8 Melt the butter in the small saucepan over low heat. Be careful not to let the butter burn. When the butter has melted, pour it into a mixing bowl.

9 Add the apples, sugar, and cinnamon to the melted butter. Mix well. Spread the apple mixture over the batter.

Step 9

10 🖐 Bake the kuchen 40 minutes. Have an adult help you poke a toothpick into the center. If the toothpick comes out clean, the kuchen is done. If not, bake 5 minutes more and test again. When done, remove from oven.

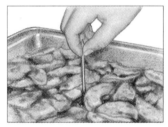

Step 10

11 With the pastry brush, spread the jelly on the apples. Serve warm, right out of the pan, with whipped cream.

Iced Fruit Tea

In Kit's time, nobody had air-conditioning. One way people kept cool was by drinking iced tea.

Ingredients

- 6 to 8 juice oranges
- 2 lemons
- 4 cups water
- 5 tea bags*
- ⅔ cup sugar
- 3 cups ginger ale
- Ice cubes

Equipment

- Sharp knife
- Cutting board
- Juicer
- Measuring cup
- Mixing bowl
- Teakettle
- Large teapot
- Wooden spoon
- Strainer to fit pitcher
- Pitcher

Serves 6–8

Orange spice tea or fruity herb teas work well.

1. Have an adult help you cut 3 2½-inch strips of orange rind. Then cut the oranges in half.

Step 1

2. Squeeze the juice out of the orange halves by turning them back and forth on the juicer while pushing down. Pour the juice into the measuring cup. Keep going until you have 2 cups of juice. Pour the juice into the mixing bowl.

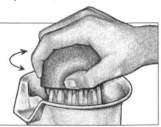

Step 2

3. Cut the lemons in half. Squeeze the juice out of the lemons. Measure out ½ cup of fresh lemon juice. Add it to the bowl. (Don't worry about the seeds.)

Step 3

4. Pour the water into the teakettle. Place the kettle over high heat.

5. Put the tea bags in the large teapot. When the water in the kettle boils, pour it over the tea bags.

6 Put the orange rind in the teapot with the tea. Add the sugar. Let the tea mixture *steep,* or sit, for about 7 minutes. Then stir the tea to make sure the sugar is dissolved.

7 Place the strainer over the pitcher. Pour the orange and lemon juice through the strainer into the pitcher.

8 Carefully pour the tea through the strainer into the pitcher. Chill the mixture.

Step 8

9 When you are ready to serve the tea, add the ginger ale. Pour the mixture into tall glasses filled with ice cubes. Cut thin slices of orange, and float an orange slice in each glass.

Backyard Games

Kit did chores in her backyard, such as feeding the chickens and hanging the laundry, but the backyard was a place to have fun, too. Sometimes laundry baskets and clothespins even came in handy for games. Using them to play a game like Roll Ball was a lot more fun for Kit than using them to do the boarders' laundry!

Roll Ball

Players stand side by side, with a laundry basket lying on its side in front of each girl. The first player stands 15 feet away, facing the others. She has three chances to roll a ball into a basket. (Use a large soft ball, such as a soccer ball or volleyball.) If she misses, she clips a clothespin to her own basket, and the next girl in line rolls the ball. When the ball goes into a basket, everyone runs, except the girl who owns the basket—she grabs the ball and tries to tag a runner by throwing the ball at her. If she succeeds, she clips a clothespin onto the tagged runner's basket. If she fails, she clips a clothespin to her own basket. The game repeats with the next girl in line rolling the ball. When a girl has five clothespins on her basket, she's out! The last player left wins.

Barnyard Confusion

The players stand in a circle around one player, who is blindfolded. The blindfolded girl spins three times, then points to a player in the circle and asks her to make a noise like a turkey, goat, donkey, or other barnyard animal. The blind player has two chances to guess who the noisemaker is. If she fails, she takes another turn. If her guess is right, she switches places with the noisemaker, who puts on the blindfold and becomes the new guesser. Kit would have been good at this game if anyone asked her to make a noise like a chicken!

Tag and Sing

This game is like regular Tag, with a musical twist. If a runner is about to be tagged, she may earn safety by singing a song. When It turns away to chase another player, the singing may stop, but then the player is no longer safe. Players may not sing the same song twice or sing a song another player has used—if they do, they are not safe and It may tag them. A tagged player becomes the new It.

I Say Stoop

Try this funny variation on Simon Says. One girl, the Leader, faces the other players. When she says "I say stoop," the other players must stoop down. When she says "I say stand," the others must stand. Sometimes the Leader acts out her commands correctly—but sometimes she will *stand* as she says "I say stoop" and *stoop* as she says "I say stand." The others must do as the Leader *says*, not as she *does*. When a player makes a mistake, she sits down. The faster the Leader gives orders, the more mistakes players will make! The last girl standing is the new Leader.

Radio Night

On cold winter evenings, Mother served a warm, filling supper like Cincinnati chili, with bread pudding for dessert. After supper, Kit switched on the radio, and everyone pitched in to help wash the dishes. Dad and Kit sang along to their favorite songs. With the radio playing, washing up felt more like a party than a chore, and the work seemed to go faster.

When the dishes were done, Kit and Stirling might start a jigsaw puzzle, make a marble maze, or practice yo-yo tricks. If the Cincinnati Reds baseball team had played that day, Kit would listen to the news to see if the Reds had won. Then she might tune in to a suspenseful radio drama. Playing games and listening to the radio, Kit and Stirling could forget the troubles of the Depression for a few happy hours.

Create a Radio Show

You and your friends can create an old-time radio program using a cassette player, boom box, or computer.

Write a Script

Think up a dramatic situation. The characters could be people you know, people you made up, or characters from a book or TV show. The situation might be a mystery to solve or a challenge to overcome. Write out the *dialogue,* or lines that each character says. Make sure each line moves the plot along! Remember, the audience will not be able to see you act, so the dialogue must tell the listener what's happening.

Assign Roles

With your friends, decide who will read each part. The nice thing about doing a radio show is that one person can read more than one part. And you don't have to memorize any lines!

Create Sound Effects

The *foley artist,* or sound-effects person, has one of the most important roles in a radio show. The foley artist chooses background music to set the atmosphere, and sound effects to make a show seem realistic. Try these tricks to create different sounds:

- **Rain**—*Drop grains of rice slowly into an aluminum pie pan. If it's a downpour, drop the rice faster!*
- **Wind**—*Blow softly into the microphone.*
- **Car motor**—*Run a blender or electric mixer at slow speed, several feet from the microphone.*
- **Gunshot**—*Whack a yardstick against a table, or clack two wooden boards together.*
- **Fire**—*Crinkle cellophane or tissue paper next to the microphone.*
- **Hoofbeats**—*Turn two cups upside down and clop them on the tabletop.*
- **Opening a safe**—*Twist the dial of a combination lock.*

Set the Scene

Create the right mood with background music and sound effects as each scene opens. Are your characters at a party? Play a few seconds of rowdy dance tunes. At a fancy restaurant? Play quiet classical music and clink silverware on dishes. In a graveyard? Play spooky music, or make the sounds of wind and hooting owls.

Put It All Together

Practice reading the script aloud a few times, and then record your show. Announce the title at the beginning, over suitable background music. If you make a mistake, just back up and re-record over the mistake. When you're all done, play your radio program for your friends and family.

The Golden Age of Radio

In the days before television, families listened to the radio for entertainment. There were dramas, comedies, cooking shows, and detective series, just as there are now on TV. Kit's mother might have listened to a popular drama called *Ma Perkins*. A resourceful woman bringing her family through the Depression, Ma Perkins always had a positive outlook, even in the face of difficulties. Kit and her friends would have tuned in to kids' shows like *Little Orphan Annie*, about a penniless orphan adopted by a billionaire. In the 1930s, when most people were poor, children liked to imagine suddenly being rich!

Cincinnati Chili

Ingredients

Chili:
- 2 pounds ground beef
- 2 medium onions
- 1 tablespoon vinegar
- 2 tablespoons chili powder
- 2 teaspoons ground cumin
- ½ teaspoon garlic powder
- ¼ teaspoon cayenne pepper* (optional)
- One 15-ounce can tomato sauce
- 1 cup water

Sweet spices:
- 1 teaspoon cinnamon
- 1 teaspoon allspice
- 1 teaspoon unsweet-ened cocoa

Noodles:
- 6 cups water
- 1 pound spaghetti

Equipment

- Large soup pot with cover
- Wooden spoon
- Colander
- Large bowl
- Measuring cups and spoons
- Sharp knife
- Cutting board
- Large saucepan with cover

* Use only if you like hot, spicy food!

Serves 6–8

Cincinnati chili was invented by a Greek immigrant. He used sweet spices in his recipe. You might want to make the recipe without those spices first, then add them next time if you're feeling adventurous!

1 Crumble the beef into the large soup pot. With the heat on medium-high, stir and cook the meat until it is brown.

2 Set the colander in the large bowl. Have an adult help you pour the meat in the colander to drain the fat. Pour the meat back in the pot and return it to the stove. Later, when the meat fat in the bowl hardens, put it in the garbage.

Step 3

3 With an adult's help, peel and chop the onions. Add them to the pot.

4 Add the vinegar, chili powder, cumin, garlic powder, and cayenne pepper.* Stir and cook 5 minutes. Add the tomato sauce and water. If you want, add the cinnamon, allspice, and cocoa.

Step 4

5 Cover the pot and bring the chili to a boil. Then turn the heat to low and let the chili *simmer*, or bubble gently, for an hour. Stir occasionally.

6 Twenty minutes before you serve the chili, cook the spaghetti. Pour 6 cups of water into the saucepan. Cover the pan and set it on high heat.

7 When the water boils, add the spaghetti and turn the heat to medium. Boil the spaghetti for 8 to 10 minutes. While the spaghetti cooks, wash the colander.

8 Have an adult help you pour the spaghetti into the colander at the sink. Rinse the spaghetti with cool water, then put it back in the pan.

Tomato Cousin

Chili peppers are related to tomatoes. They can be used fresh, or dried and then ground into a spicy powder.

Step 8

9 Serve the chili over the spaghetti. Try these Cincinnati-style combos:

3-Way Chili
Top with grated cheddar cheese.

4-Way Chili
Add a spoonful of chopped sweet onions before the cheese.

5-Way Chili
Add a spoonful of cooked red beans with the onions and cheese.

Or do what Kit and her friends did— spoon the chili over hot dogs!

Bread Pudding

Instead of throwing out stale bread, use it to make this delicious dessert. "Waste not, want not," as Aunt Millie would say!

Ingredients

- Softened butter
- 7 thick slices white bread
- 3 eggs
- 4 cups milk
- ½ cup sugar
- ¼ teaspoon salt
- ½ cup raisins
- 1 teaspoon vanilla
- ½ teaspoon cinnamon
- Cream

Equipment

- Baking dish with lid (or use aluminum foil)
- Butter knife
- Mixing bowl
- Fork
- Measuring cups and spoons
- Wooden spoon
- Potholders

Serves 6–8

1 Preheat the oven to 325°. Grease the baking dish with butter. Set it aside.

2 Spread butter thickly on each bread slice. Cut the slices in half, then line the bottom and sides of the baking dish with the bread, buttered-side up. Set any remaining bread slices aside.

Step 2

3 Crack the eggs into the mixing bowl. Beat them with the fork.

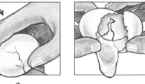

Step 3

4 Add the milk, sugar, salt, raisins, vanilla, and cinnamon. Mix well, then pour the mixture over the bread.

5 Place any remaining bread slices on top, and press them down so that they are covered with the liquid. Let the bread pudding soak for 10 minutes.

Step 5

6 Cover the dish and bake the pudding for 30 minutes. Then uncover the dish and bake it for another 30 minutes.

7 Have an adult take the dish out of the oven. Serve warm with a little cream poured on top.

Bread Lines and Milk Lines

Bread was inexpensive, healthful, and filling, so soup kitchens gave out loaves to people in need. Some places also provided milk for children. These girls are carrying their free milk back home in buckets.

Baseball Pennant

Make your pennant in the colors of your favorite team. It doesn't have to be baseball—you can cheer on your soccer or swim team!

Materials

- Piece of felt, at least 9 by 24 inches
- Scissors
- Yardstick
- Piece of tracing paper
- Pencil
- Straight pins
- Large felt squares
- Glue
- Heavy books
- Dowel

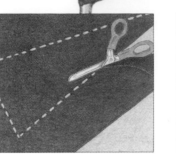

1 Cut a pennant shape (a thin triangle) from the piece of felt. The short side should be 9 inches, and the long sides should be 24 inches.

2 Trace the letter patterns shown on page 93 onto tracing paper. Cut out the letters.

3 Pin the letters to squares of felt, and cut around the letters. Unpin the patterns.

Kit didn't let school clothes stop her from sliding in for a home run!

4 Arrange the felt letters on the pennant. Glue the letters into place. Put books on top of the letters until the glue dries.

5 Glue the dowel to the back of the pennant. Let it dry. Now cheer for your team!

America's Pastime

Many of baseball's biggest stars, such as Babe Ruth, Lou Gehrig, and Joe DiMaggio, played in the 1930s. Fans followed the teams in the newspaper and on the radio, which had just begun broadcasting baseball games live. Kids collected and traded cards of their favorite players. Girls and boys also loved playing baseball themselves, especially since many of them could not afford to attend professional ball games. A bat, a ball, and a vacant lot were all they needed for an afternoon of glorious fun.

Yo-Yo

Yo-yos were popular with both children and adults in the 1930s. They were cheap and easy to make, and they could be played with almost anywhere.

Materials

- 2 craft disks, 2½ by ½ inches*
- Newspaper
- Acrylic paint
- Paintbrush
- Flat-head plug, ½ inch*
- Wood glue
- String or cord

*Available in craft shops

1 Place the flat sides of the craft disks on the newspaper. Paint the disks, then let them dry for 15 minutes. Add a second coat of paint. If you like, turn the disks over and paint the flat sides, too.

2 When the paint is dry, glue the plug to the center of the flat side of one of the disks. Let the glue dry.

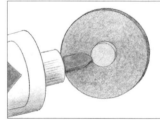

Step 2

3 Glue the plug to the other disk. Let the glue dry.

4 Tie one end of the string or cord around the center of the yo-yo. Tie the other end loosely around your finger to make a loop.

Step 4

5 Wind the string or cord around the yo-yo, and it's ready for action!

Jigsaw Puzzle

In Kit's time, puzzles were so popular that there were even puzzle libraries, where you could check out a puzzle and then return it after you had finished it.

Materials

- A picture from an old magazine, calendar, or greeting card
- Foam core board
- Sponge
- Craft glue
- Rolling pin
- Pencil
- X-Acto knife

1 ✋ Have an adult use the knife to trim your picture and the foam core board to the same size.

2 Use the sponge to spread glue evenly over one side of the foam core board. Lay the picture on top. Smooth out any bubbles with the rolling pin. Let dry.

Step 2

3 Turn the foam core over and draw curvy lines on the back. Keep drawing until the blank areas are about an inch wide.

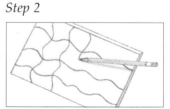

Step 3

4 ✋ Have an adult cut along all the lines with the X-Acto knife. Then turn your pieces over, and put your puzzle back together!

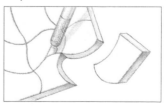

Step 4

53

Marble Maze

*Running this maze
is trickier than it looks.
Practice will pay off!*

Materials

- Tracing paper
- Pencil
- Chinet dinner plate
- Tape
- X-Acto knife
- Newspaper
- Acrylic paints
- Foam paintbrush,
  1 inch wide
- Small artist's
  paintbrush
- Permanent marker
- Marble

1 Use the tracing paper to trace the marble maze pattern on page 91.

2 Place the pattern on the inside of the plate and tape it in place. Have an adult cut out the shaded areas of the pattern with the X-Acto knife.

Step 2

3 Set the plate on the newspaper. Paint one side. Let the paint dry for at least 15 minutes. Add a second coat if necessary.

4 Paint the other side of the plate. Let it dry. If you like, paint a border around the edge of your maze. Let it dry.

5 Use the marker to write numbers by the triangles, as shown.

6 To play, place the marble in the triangle with the star underneath. Guide your marble around the maze counterclockwise, letting it roll into each triangle as you go by. Add up the points for each triangle your marble rolls into—but don't let your marble fall into the curved lines around the center triangle, or your turn is over!

Up in the Attic

After school, Kit and her friends often played in the attic—which also happened to be Kit's bedroom. At first, Kit wasn't sure she would like having her bedroom in the attic. But once she made special places for all her interests—baseball, reading, writing, and Robin Hood—it didn't seem half bad. Best of all, in a crowded house full of boarders, the attic made a great getaway spot for Kit and her friends. Up there they could eat snacks, play noisy games, and do messy crafts without bothering the boarders, especially persnickety Mrs. Howard!

Oatmeal Raisin Cookies

Oatmeal cookies make a tasty and nutritious after-school snack.

Ingredients

- ½ pound butter, softened
- 1 cup brown sugar
- ½ cup white sugar
- 2 eggs
- 1 teaspoon vanilla
- 1½ cups flour
- 1 teaspoon baking soda
- 1 teaspoon cinnamon
- ½ teaspoon salt
- 3 cups rolled oats
- 1 cup raisins

Equipment

- Measuring cups and spoons
- 2 large mixing bowls
- Electric mixer
- Rubber spatula
- Sifter
- Wooden spoon
- Teaspoon
- Cookie sheets
- Potholder
- Spatula
- Wire cooling racks

1 Preheat the oven to 350°. Measure the butter and sugars into a mixing bowl.

2 Have an adult help you use the electric mixer to beat the butter and sugar until creamy.

3 Add the eggs and vanilla. Beat well. Stop the mixer once or twice and use the rubber spatula to scrape down the sides of the bowl.

Step 3

4 Put the sifter into the other mixing bowl. Measure the flour, baking soda, cinnamon, and salt into the sifter, and sift them into the bowl.

Step 4

5  Add the sifted ingredients gradually to the butter mixture, mixing with the electric mixer after each addition.

6 Stir in the oats and the raisins with the wooden spoon. Mix well.

7 Use the teaspoon to drop the dough onto cookie sheets. Set the spoonfuls of dough 3 inches apart.

8 Bake the cookies for 10 minutes, or until the edges are golden. With an adult, take cookie sheets out of the oven.

9 Let the cookies cool for 1 minute on the cookie sheets, then use the spatula to place them on a wire rack to cool.

Kitchen Fun

These 1930s girls look ready to cook up some serious fun. The little oven on the counter was a toy that could really heat food, though it probably did not get hot enough for baking.

59

Checkerboard Sandwiches

This simple sandwich makes an eye-catching snack for a party or sleepover.

Ingredients

- 4 ounces cream cheese, softened
- 2 tablespoons of your favorite jam or jelly
- 4 slices white bread
- 4 slices dark bread

Equipment

- Mixing bowl
- Whisk
- Butter knife
- Measuring cups and spoons
- Sharp knife
- Cutting board

Serves 4

1 Put the cream cheese and the jam or jelly in the mixing bowl. Use the whisk to mix them together.

2 Spread each piece of dark bread with the cream cheese mixture, using the butter knife. Then place the white bread on top to make 4 sandwiches.

3 Stack 2 sandwiches as shown. With the sharp knife, trim off the crusts so that the sandwiches are square-shaped.

4 Separate the sandwiches. Cut each sandwich into four small squares. Arrange the squares into a checkerboard pattern.

5 Repeat steps 3 and 4 with the other 2 sandwiches. Keep the sandwiches in the refrigerator until you serve them.

Step 1

Step 3

Vanilla Milk Shake

You may need a spoon to eat this super-thick homemade shake!

Ingredients

- 6 scoops vanilla ice cream
- 1 teaspoon vanilla extract
- ½ cup milk

Equipment

- Ice cream scoop
- Measuring cups and spoons
- Blender
- Tall glasses

Serves 2

1 Scoop the ice cream into the blender. Add the vanilla and the milk.

2 Blend the ingredients for at least 1 minute, or until they are well mixed. Then pour the shake into chilled glasses.

3 To make other flavors, skip the vanilla extract. Instead, add 1 tablespoon of chocolate, caramel, or berry-flavored syrup. Or use strawberry or chocolate ice cream in place of vanilla ice cream.

Vanilla Beans

Vanilla extract is made from the pod-shaped fruit of the vanilla orchid, a flowering vine.

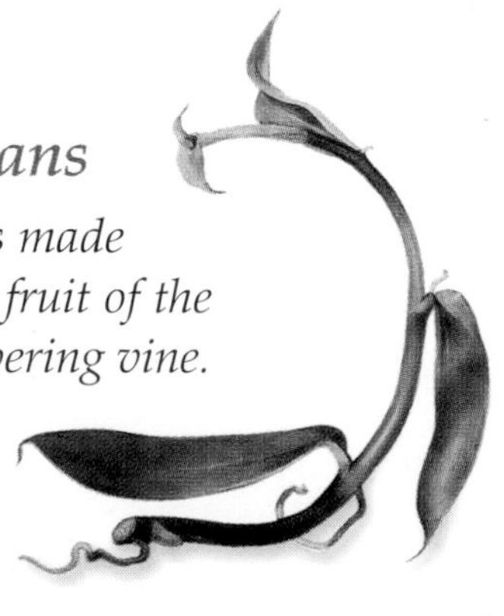

Scottie Pillow

Scottie dogs were all the rage in the 1930s because President Franklin Roosevelt had a pet Scottie.

Materials

- Pencil
- Tracing paper
- Scissors
- Straight pins
- 3 pieces of black felt, 12 by 15 inches
- Black thread
- Needle
- Scraps of red and blue felt
- Fabric glue
- Googly eye
- Two bows or buttons
- Polyester stuffing

1 Use the pencil to trace the Scottie dog pattern shown on page 92 onto tracing paper three times. Cut out the patterns.

2 Cut one pattern along dotted line 1. Throw away the front part of the pattern. Cut another pattern along dotted line 2. Throw away the back part of the pattern. Leave the third pattern whole.

Step 2

3 Pin the patterns to the black felt pieces. Cut out the shapes. Unpin the patterns.

4 Pin the two dog halves to the whole Scottie dog, matching the edges. The halves will overlap in the middle. (This is the back of the pillow, where the stuffing will go in.)

Step 4

5 Cut an 18-inch piece of thread, and thread the needle. Tie a double knot at the other end of the thread.

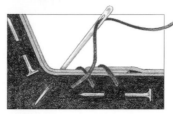

6 Use the whipstitch on page 5 to sew the Scotties together around the outer edge. When you near the end of the thread, tie a knot by your last stitch and cut off the extra thread. Then repeat steps 5 and 6 to sew all the way around the Scottie.

Step 6

7 Use the pencil to trace the jacket and the nose patterns shown on page 92 onto tracing paper. Cut out the patterns.

8 Pin the nose pattern to the red felt. Pin the jacket pattern to the blue felt. Cut out the nose and the jacket. Set aside.

Step 9

9 Cut a piece of thread and thread the needle. Tie a double knot at the other end of the thread. Sew the bows or buttons onto the jacket.

Step 10

10 Use the fabric glue to glue the eye, the nose, and the jacket to the Scottie dog.

11 Once the glue has dried, fill the dog with the stuffing, then stitch it closed.

Step 11

FDR and Fala
Franklin Roosevelt's Scottie, Fala, made many public appearances.

Lamp Shade

Cast a warm glow with this easy craft. It's a clever way to give new life to an old lamp.

Materials

- Tissue paper, 4 colors (the two background colors should be lighter)
- Ruler
- Scissors
- Small lamp with white shade
- Mod Podge*
- Foam paintbrush, 1 inch wide

* Available at craft stores.

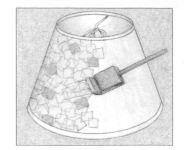

1 Cut the background-color tissue paper into strips about 1 inch wide. Cut each strip into 1-inch squares.

2 Paint a layer of Mod Podge on a section of the shade. Place the squares in the background colors on the shade. Let the colors overlap.

3 Paint Mod Podge over the squares to glue them to the shade. Repeat steps 2 and 3 until the shade is covered with squares.

4 Rinse the paintbrush in warm water and let it dry. Let the shade dry overnight.

5 Use the other 2 colors of tissue paper to make a design on the shade. Cut out circles and petals to form flowers, or make up your own design. Glue the design onto the shade with Mod Podge. Let it dry overnight.

To avoid overheating your lamp, use only a 40-watt bulb, or else switch the lamp off when you leave the room.

Bright Lights, Big Country

In Kit's time, cities and towns had electricity, but many *rural*, or country, areas did not. Electric companies couldn't afford to run wires across miles and miles of countryside just to serve a few farms. In 1935 President Franklin Roosevelt created the Rural Electrification Administration to provide farms with electricity. It took decades to run wires around the entire U.S., but by the early 1970s, almost every farm had electricity. Many farm families still recall the thrill of switching on a light for the first time!

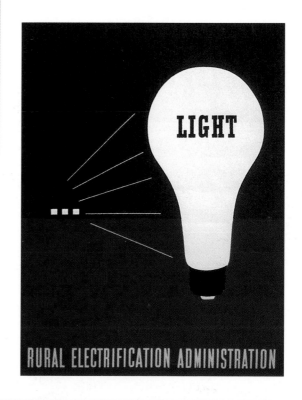

LIGHT

RURAL ELECTRIFICATION ADMINISTRATION

Tommy-Walkers

Step up to new heights! These stilts are much easier to walk on than the kind made from poles. Clomp, stomp, here we come!

Materials

- 2 empty cans, 28 ounces, with labels removed
- Softened clay
- Brad-awl or hammer and nail
- Acrylic paints in 2 colors
- Newspaper
- Foam paintbrush, 1 inch wide
- Yardstick
- Twine
- Scissors
- Tape

1 Place small balls of clay on opposite sides of each can, near the top. With an adult's help, use the brad-awl or the hammer and nail to pierce holes through the clay and can. Remove the clay.

Step 1

2 Set the cans on newspaper. Use the foam paintbrush to paint the sides of the cans. Rinse the paintbrush.

3 Let the cans dry for at least 20 minutes. After the paint is dry, add a second coat if necessary. Let the paint dry.

4 Paint the tops of the cans using the second color. Let the cans dry, then add a second coat if necessary.

5 Once the paint is dry, stand on the cans. Hold your arms straight down, and have an adult measure the distance from your palms to the floor. Cut the twine so that it is twice the length that you measured.

Step 5

6 Put a piece of tape on each end of the twine. Roll the tape tightly to form stiff tips, like the ends of a shoelace. Thread the ends of the twine through the holes in each can. Tie the ends together in a double knot inside the can.

Step 6

7 Then stand on your stilts, grab the twine loops, and walk tall!

Paper Bx

A perfect place for tiny treasures, this clever box is based on Japanese paper-folding designs. It needs no glue or staples to hold together.

Materials

- 2 pieces of stiff paper, 12 by 12 inches*
- Ruler
- Pencil
- Scissors

Heavy wrapping paper or wallpaper (un-pre-pasted) works well.

1 Lay the paper on the table with the back side facing up.

2 Use the ruler to draw a line on the paper from 1 corner to the opposite corner. Draw another line from the other corner to its opposite. The 2 lines should make an X.

Step 2

3 Fold in the 4 corners so that they meet in the center.

Step 3

4 Fold in 1 side to meet the center of the X. Fold in the opposite side to meet the center of the X. Unfold the 2 sides, leaving 2 creases.

Step 4

5 Repeat step 4 with the other 2 sides. The paper should appear as shown.

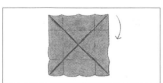
Step 5

6 Make 4 cuts, 2 on each side, as shown. The cuts should be on the creases and should stop when you reach the next crease. Then lift out the triangular flaps on the 2 sides.

Step 6

7 Stand the other 2 sides up and fold in the squares on the ends, as shown.

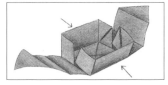
Step 7

8 Fold down the first 2 sides so that the triangular points are back in the center. This is the top of the box.

Step 8

9 To make the bottom of the box, trim the second piece of paper so that it is 11¾ inches on each side. Then repeat steps 2 through 8.

Treasures from the Orient

People in the 1930s liked tableware and trinkets from the Orient, because they were exotic and interesting—and inexpensive. The countries of Asia were known as "the Orient" in Kit's time.

Desk Blotter

Whether you like to write postcards or poetry, having a blotter on your desk will make your writing feel more important.

Materials

- Pencil
- Ruler
- 2 large sheets of heavy paper, at least 15 by 20 inches
- Poster board, 15 by 20 inches
- Small sheet of heavy paper, at least 5 by 8 inches
- Scissors
- Foam paintbrush
- Glue or glue stick
- Rolling pin

1 Measure and trim 1 sheet of paper so that it is 15 by 20 inches.

2 Use the foam brush to spread glue on one side of the paper. Press the paper onto the poster board. Use the rolling pin to roll out any air bubbles. Let dry.

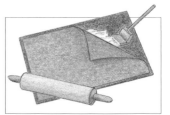

Step 2

3 Measure and trim the other sheet of paper so that it is 14 by 19 inches.

4 Center this sheet on the first paper, and glue it down. Roll out any air bubbles.

5 Cut out 4 strips of paper, 2 by 5 inches each.

6 To form the corners of your blotter, place each strip across a corner of the board. Fold the ends of each strip behind the board and glue them down.

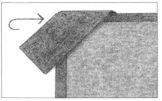

Step 6

Pencil Holder

Make several of these handy holders to organize your pens, scissors, and markers. For storing paper clips and rubber bands, use tuna cans!

Materials

- Empty 15-ounce can with label removed
- Tape measure
- Ribbon, about 1½ inches wide
- Scissors
- Fabric glue
- Ribbon, about ⅞ inch wide

1 Measure around the can. Add 1 inch to the length you measured.

2 Measure and cut out 3 pieces of the wide ribbon to the length from step 1.

3 Glue the pieces of ribbon at the top, middle, and bottom of the can. Line up the cut ends of ribbon. The ends will overlap. If you like, fold the top end of each ribbon under to hide the raw edge.

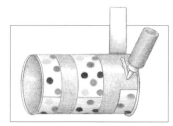

Step 3

4 Measure and cut out 2 pieces of the medium ribbon to the length from step 1.

5 Glue the ribbons to the can, covering the edges of the first ribbons. Line up the cut ends with the first ribbons, and fold the top ends under, if you like (see step 3).

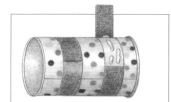

Step 5

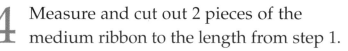

71

Antics in the Attic

On rainy days, Kit and her friends escaped to the attic. There they hatched plots and played indoor games. You can play these games just as Kit did, using things you have around the house.

Button Race

Kit's Aunt Millie probably had a big button collection. See if your mother or grand-mother has one that you can use for this game. Give each player 25 buttons and a piece of heavy thread 18 inches long. Who can thread all her buttons the fastest?

Do This, Do That

If you like charades, you'll enjoy this performing game. One player is the Commander. She writes commands on slips of paper, such as "sing a song," "do a handstand," "make a funny face," and so on. Then she folds the papers and places them in a bag. The other players take turns drawing a slip and obeying the commands. After everyone performs, the players vote on who carried out her command in the best style. The winner becomes the new Commander, and the game starts again.

Alphabet Traveling

This game gets harder as you go along! Everyone sits in a circle. The first player turns to the girl on her right and says, "I am going by **a**irplane to **A**frica." The other girl asks, "What will you do there?" The first player replies, "**A**sk **a**dvice" or "**A**ct **a**pe-like" or any action beginning with A. The girl on her right then announces that she is going somewhere beginning with B, such as "I am going to **B**oston by **b**oat." The game continues around the circle, moving down the alphabet.

Japanese Fan Race

When it got hot up in the attic, Kit and Ruthie kept cool by playing this fun fan game. Give each girl a 3-inch square of tissue paper, marked with her name, and a hand-held fan. (The fans may simply be pieces of paper pleated like an accordion and then stapled at one end.) At the other side of the room, set up a goal, such as two books placed a foot apart. On the word "Go," each player tries to fan her tissue paper through the goal first.

Game Time

Board games were all the rage in 1932. Department stores opened game departments to serve eager shoppers. Kids enjoyed classics like Chinese Checkers and Parcheesi as well as new games. "Coast to Coast Air Race," below, was a puzzle game inspired by the popularity of daring young pilots such as Amelia Earhart and Charles Lindbergh.

73

Care and Share

When the hard times hit, Kit found creative ways to help her family. Soon she began to see that other families needed even more help than her own. Some people didn't have food to feed their pets. Some families didn't even have a place to live. Kit, Ruthie, and Stirling donated food and clothing, and they spread the word about families in need. Kit found that helping others made her feel just as good as helping her own family.

You and your friends can help a family in your community. Offer to do laundry or cleaning for a neighbor with a new baby. Bring a hot meal to a new family in your neighborhood. You'll feel great—and you'll make new friends!

Flour-Sack Napkin

In the 1930s, flour came in white cloth sacks. To make napkins, Kit just cut an empty sack into squares and stitched a design on each one.

Materials
- Dark marker
- Tracing paper
- Masking tape
- Woven napkin, white or light-colored
- Fabric marker
- Embroidery hoop, 4 inches wide
- Embroidery floss
- Embroidery needle
- Scissors

1 With the dark marker, trace the cat pattern shown on page 77 onto tracing paper. (Or, if you prefer, draw your own design. Keep it simple!)

2 Tape the tracing paper to a bright window. Tape the napkin over the paper, so the design shows through one corner of the napkin.

3 Use the fabric marker to trace the design onto the napkin. Take the napkin off the window.

Step 3

4 Take the embroidery hoop apart by loosening the screw. Place the napkin over the inner hoop so that the design lies inside the hoop.

5 Snap the outer hoop over the fabric and inner hoop, and then tighten the screw.

Steps 4 and 5

6 Cut an 18-inch piece of floss. The floss is made up of 6 strands, but to embroider, you use only 2 strands. Separate 2 strands.

Step 6

7 Thread the needle with the 2 strands. Tie a double knot at the other end of the floss.

8 Embroider your design with a chain stitch. Push the needle through the back of the fabric and come up at A. Then put the needle back in at A, next to where you came up, leaving a small loop of thread.

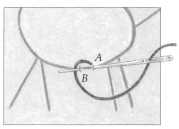
Steps 8 and 9

9 Bring the needle out at B and through the loop of thread. Pull the thread snug.

10 Put the needle back in at B, next to where you came up, leaving a small thread loop. Continue stitching around the cat's body.

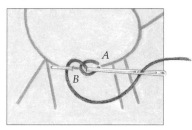
Step 10

11 To finish, make a tiny stitch over the last loop. Tie a knot on the back of the napkin at your last stitch. Cut off the extra thread.

12 Repeat steps 6 through 11 to stitch the rest of the cat. Remove the embroidery hoop.

Hobo Code

A cat design was a code among hoboes for "kind woman lives here." Drawn on a fence or wall, it meant hoboes could stop at that house for a meal.

Glazed Carrots

Kit's mother liked this dish because it brightened her table and used vegetables from the garden.

Ingredients

- 1 pound baby carrots
- 2 cups water
- 3 lemons
- 3 tablespoons butter
- 2 tablespoons light brown sugar
- 2 tablespoons orange marmalade
- ¼ teaspoon salt
- ⅛ teaspoon pepper

Equipment

- Saucepan with lid
- Colander
- Sharp knife
- Cutting board
- Juicer
- Teaspoon
- Measuring cups and spoons
- Wooden spoon

Serves 6–8

1 Put the carrots and water in the saucepan. Cover the pan and place it over medium heat. Bring the water to a boil.

2 Let the carrots *simmer*, or cook gently, for about 10 minutes. They should be just tender, not soft.

3 Place the colander in the sink. Have an adult help you pour the carrots into the colander to drain. Then put the carrots back in the saucepan.

Step 3

4 Have an adult help you slice the lemon in half with the sharp knife.

Step 4

5 Squeeze the juice out of the lemon halves by pressing them on the juicer and twisting back and forth. Remove seeds with the teaspoon. Repeat steps 4 and 5 until you have ¼ cup of juice.

Step 5

6 Add the lemon juice to the carrots. Stir in the butter, brown sugar, marmalade, salt, and pepper. Leave the saucepan uncovered.

7 Set the heat on low and let the carrots simmer for 20 minutes. Stir the carrots often until they become *glazed*, or coated with the orange sauce. Serve warm.

Step 7

Baked Macaroni and Cheese

Don't let the length of this recipe fool you—it's quite easy, and much tastier than mac and cheese from a box.

Ingredients

- 1 stick butter
- 8 ounces (or 2 cups) macaroni noodles
- 2¼ cups milk
- 4 tablespoons flour
- ½ teaspoon salt
- ¼ teaspoon pepper
- 2 cups grated cheddar cheese
- ½ cup bread crumbs

Equipment

- Large casserole dish
- Large saucepan
- Measuring cups and spoons
- Wooden spoon
- Colander
- 2 medium saucepans
- Small skillet
- Potholders

Serves 4

1 Preheat the oven to 375°. Grease the casserole dish with 1 tablespoon of butter. Set it aside.

2 Pour 2 quarts of water into the large saucepan. Cover the pan and set it over high heat. Bring the water to a boil.

3 Add the noodles. Turn the heat to medium. Boil the noodles for 8 minutes, stirring occasionally.

4 Set the colander in the sink. Have an adult help you pour the noodles into the colander. Rinse the noodles with cold water and put them back into the pan. Set the pan aside.

Step 4

5 In a saucepan, heat the milk on medium-high. Stir constantly until steaming hot, but not boiling. Remove from heat.

6 In the other saucepan, melt 4 tablespoons of butter over low heat. Be careful not to let it burn. When the butter is melted, stir in the flour, salt, and pepper.

7 Add the hot milk to the butter mixture. Turn the heat to medium-high. Cook the mixture 5 minutes, stirring constantly.

8 Add 1½ cups of grated cheese. Stir the mixture until all the cheese has melted. Remove from heat.

Step 8

9 Put half the noodles into the casserole dish. Cover with half the cheese sauce. Sprinkle with ¼ cup of grated cheese. Repeat with the remaining noodles, cheese sauce, and grated cheese.

Step 10

10 Melt 2 tablespoons of butter in the skillet over low heat. Add the bread crumbs. Stir until all the crumbs are moistened.

11 Sprinkle the crumbs over the macaroni and cheese. Bake the dish uncovered for 25 minutes, or until browned on top. Have an adult take the dish out of the oven. Serve hot.

Roast Beef Hash

❀ ❀ ❀ ❀ ❀

Hash is a great way to use up leftovers. If you have meat and potatoes left over from a previous meal, just start the recipe at step 8!

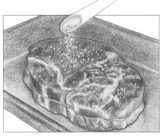

Step 1

Ingredients

- 2½ pounds beef chuck roast
- 1 teaspoon salt
- ½ teaspoon pepper
- 3 medium potatoes
- 1 medium onion
- 4 tablespoons oil
- One 12-ounce jar of beef gravy
- 1 teaspoon salt
- ½ teaspoon pepper

Equipment

- Measuring cups and spoons
- Baking pan
- Potholders
- Aluminum foil
- Vegetable peeler
- Sharp knife
- Cutting board
- Medium saucepan with lid
- Fork
- Colander
- Large skillet
- Wooden spoon

Serves 6

82

1 Preheat the oven to 350°. Sprinkle the salt and pepper evenly over the meat on all sides. Put the meat into the baking pan.

2 Have an adult put the pan on the middle oven rack. Bake 1½ hours. When the juices run clear, the meat is done.

3 Have an adult remove the pan from the oven and cover the meat with foil. Let it "rest" for 15 minutes. The meat keeps cooking as it rests and is easier to cut.

4 Peel the potatoes. With an adult's help, use the sharp knife to slice them into ½-inch cubes. Put the potatoes in the saucepan.

5 Add enough water to cover the potatoes. Cover the pan and set on high heat. When the water boils, turn the heat down.

6   Let the potatoes *simmer,* or bubble gently, for 15 minutes. After 15 minutes, poke the fork into a potato. If it goes in easily, the potatoes are done.

7   Set the colander in the sink. Have an adult help you pour the potatoes into the colander to drain.

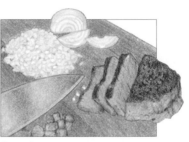

Step 7

8   With an adult's help, use the sharp knife to chop the onion. Slice the roast beef, then cut it into small cubes until you have 3 cups of beef.

Step 8

9   Place the oil in the large skillet and set it over medium heat. Put a piece of onion in the skillet, too.

10   When the onion begins to sizzle, add the rest of the onion, potatoes, beef cubes, and gravy.

11   Use the wooden spoon to stir the hash constantly. Cook it for 15 more minutes, or until it is browned. Serve hot.

Soup Kitchens

In big cities, many soup kitchens served more than 1,000 meals every day. In Chicago, even gangster Al Capone ran a soup kitchen to help feed the hungry.

83

Banana Cake

Over-ripe bananas? Don't toss them!
They'll taste delicious in this moist cake.

Ingredients

- Butter to grease baking pans
- 2¼ cups cake flour
- ½ teaspoon baking powder
- ¾ teaspoon baking soda
- ½ teaspoon salt
- ½ cup butter, softened
- 1½ cups sugar
- 2 eggs
- 5 medium bananas
- 1 teaspoon vanilla
- ¼ cup buttermilk
- Vanilla frosting

Equipment

- Two 9-inch baking pans
- Sifter
- Measuring cups and spoons
- 2 large mixing bowls
- Electric mixer
- Rubber spatula
- Small mixing bowl
- Fork
- Potholders
- Toothpick
- Wire cooling racks
- Butter knife
- Cutting board
- Sharp knife

1 Preheat the oven to 350°. Grease the baking pans with butter. Set them aside.

2 Put the sifter into a large mixing bowl. Measure the cake flour, baking powder, soda, and salt into the sifter. Sift them into the bowl. Set the bowl aside.

Step 2

3 Put ½ cup of butter into the other large mixing bowl. Have an adult help you use the electric mixer to beat the butter until it is soft.

4 Slowly add the sugar to the butter and beat until fluffy. Turn off the mixer. Scrape the sides of the bowl with the rubber spatula.

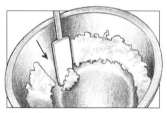
Step 4

5 Crack the eggs into the mixture. Beat well with the electric mixer.

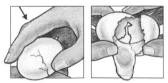
Step 5

6 Add the dry ingredients gradually, beating gently with the electric mixer.

7 Peel 3 bananas. Place them in the small mixing bowl. Mash them with the fork.

Step 7

8 Add 1 cup of mashed bananas to the mixture. Add the vanilla and the buttermilk. Beat the mixture until it is smooth. Pour it into the baking pans.

9 Bake the cakes for 30 minutes. Have an adult help you poke a toothpick into the center of one of the cakes. If the toothpick comes out clean, the cakes are done. Set them on the racks to cool.

10 With an adult's help, remove the cakes from the pans. Frost the top of one of the cakes with a butter knife. Have an adult help you slice the last 2 bananas using the sharp knife. Lay the slices on top of the frosting. Place the other cake on top of the slices. Frost the rest of the cake.

Banana Bunch
Bananas are the fruit of a fast-growing tropical plant that looks like a small palm tree.

Classroom Party

These 1930s girls made their teacher two homemade birthday cakes. Notice how every girl has the same haircut, called a "bob." With her bobbed hair, side part, and barrette, Kit was right in style!

Checkerbard

Do you know someone stuck at home or in bed? Bring over this board and match wits in a good old-fashioned game of checkers!

Materials

- Craft board, 10 by 14 inches
- Ruler
- Pencil
- Masking tape
- Acrylic paints (red, black, and yellow)
- Foam paintbrush, 1 inch wide
- Permanent marker
- Artist's paintbrush
- Tissues
- 24 buttons or coins

1 Use the ruler to measure 2 inches in from each long end of the board. Draw lines so that you have a 10-by-10-inch square in the center of the board.

Step 1

2 Put masking tape along the outsides of the lines. Paint the square red using the foam paintbrush.

Step 2

3 Let the board dry, then paint another coat of red paint. Let it dry for at least 20 minutes. Rinse the brush in water.

4 Mark off 8 lines 1¼ inches apart and 1¼ inches from the strips of tape. Then turn the ruler the other way, and repeat. You should have 8 rows of 8 squares. Each square should have 1¼-inch sides. Go over the lines with the marker.

Step 4

5 Use the artist's paintbrush to carefully paint every other square black, in a checkerboard pattern. Then paint the outer edges of the board black. Quickly blot any mistakes with a damp tissue.

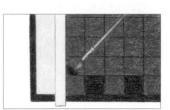

Step 5

6 Let the black paint dry. Remove the masking tape.

7 Use the yellow paint and the foam brush to paint the spaces at the sides of the grid. Let the board dry.

8 You can use buttons or coins as checkers. Collect buttons in 2 colors, 12 of each color. Or use 12 nickels and 12 pennies.

Want to Know More?

Here are some fun ways you and your friends can get an inside view of life during the Great Depression.

Read Books Set in Kit's Time

- *Bud, Not Buddy*
  by Christopher Paul Curtis

- *The Christmas Barn*
  by C. L. Davis

- *A Letter to Mrs. Roosevelt*
  by C. Coco De Young

- *Out of the Dust*
  by Karen Hesse

- *Life During the Great Depression*
  by Dennis Nishi (nonfiction)

- *A Long Way from Chicago* and
  A Year Down Yonder
  by Richard Peck

- *Children of the Dust Bowl: The True
  Story of the School at Weedpatch Camp*
  by Jerry Stanley (nonfiction)

- *Roll of Thunder, Hear My Cry*
  by Mildred D. Taylor

Bakelite Radio

In the 1930s, most radios had wooden cabinets, like the one shown on page 44. But a few radios were made of Bakelite, an early type of plastic.

Listen to Hit Songs of the 1930s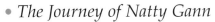

- "Brother, Can You Spare a Dime?"
- "Dream a Little Dream of Me"
- "Happy Days Are Here Again"
- "On the Sunny Side of the Street"
- "Who's Afraid of the Big Bad Wolf?"
- "Winter Wonderland"
- "Stormy Weather"

Watch Movies Set in Kit's Time

- *The Journey of Natty Gann*
- *The Grapes of Wrath*
- *Paper Moon*
- *Annie*

Visit Museums and Web Sites About the Depression Era

- Michigan Historical Center
  Great Depression Gallery
  717 W. Allegan Street
  Lansing, Michigan
  www.sos.state.mi.us/history/museum/
  explore/museums/hismus/1900-75/
  depressn/labnews2.html

- Franklin D. Roosevelt Library and Museum
  Hyde Park, New York
  www.fdrlibrary.marist.edu/

- Civilian Conservation Corps Museum
  North Higgins Lake State Park
  Grayling, Michigan
  www.sos.state.mi.us/history/museum/
  museccc/index.html

Clark Gable, Reporting

*Screen star Clark Gable posed behind the camera in a publicity photo for the 1938 film **Too Hot to Handle**, in which he plays a newsreel reporter.*

Clutch Purse

Marble Maze

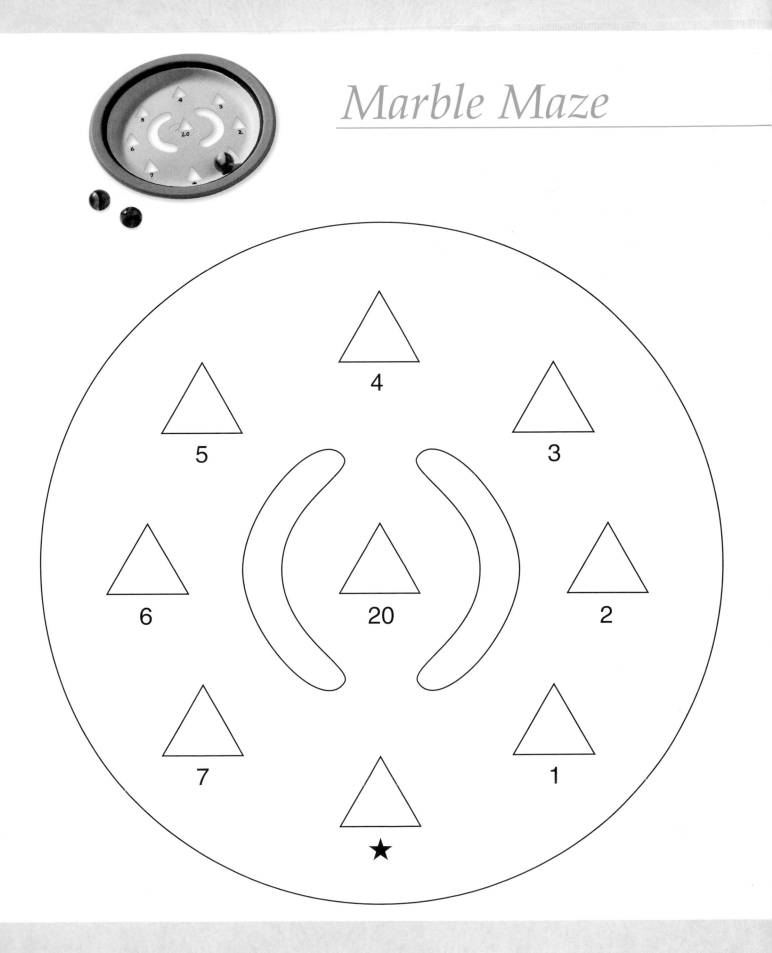

Scottie Pillow

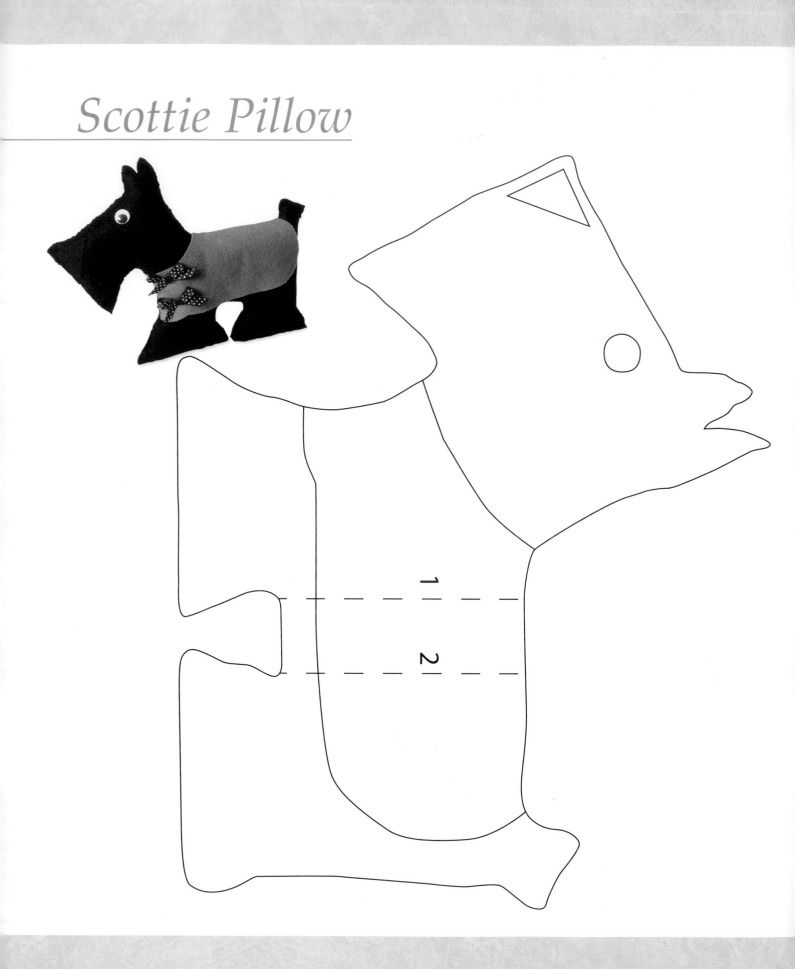

1

2

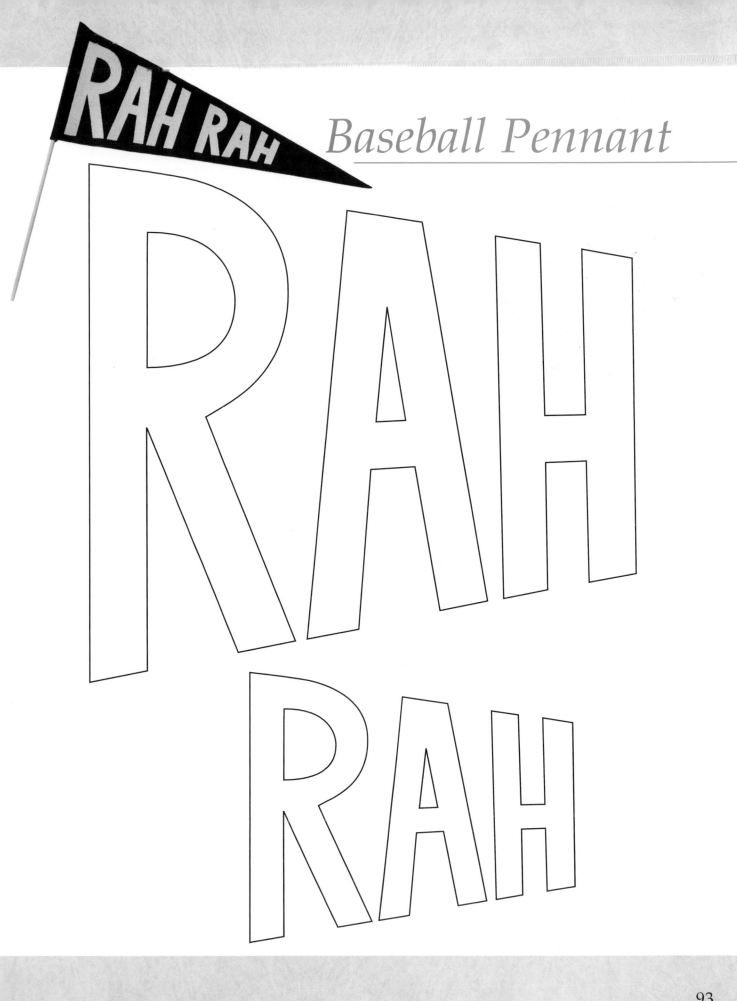

Baseball Pennant

Published by Pleasant Company Publications

Visit our Web site at **americangirl.com**

02 03 04 05 06 07 08 09 QWD 10 9 8 7 6 5 4 3 2

American Girl®, The American Girls Collection®, Kit Kittredge®and Kit®
are trademarks of Pleasant Company.

Questions or comments?
Call 1-800-845-0005 or write to
Customer Service, American Girl, 8400 Fairway Place, Middleton, WI 53562.

PICTURE CREDITS
The following individuals and organizations have generously given permission to
reprint images in this book:
p. 7—boarding house, courtesy of Doris Deaton; p. 8—pickup truck, Library of Congress; girls in
tree, Minnesota Historical Society; p. 9—feed-sack dresses, family of Muriel Church; selling eggs, J.C.
Allen and Son, Inc.; rollerskating, FPG International; p. 19—pushcart, Bettmann/CORBIS; p. 23—
corn husk mats, Library of Congress; p. 31—waiting in line, Library of Congress; p. 32—apple press,
J.C. Allen and Son, Inc.; p. 45—radio, printed with permission of Emerson Radio Corp.; Orphan
Annie poster, Little Orphan Annie ® & © Tribune Media Services, Inc.; p. 49—soup kitchen,
National Archives; girls with pails, Library of Congress; p. 51—playing baseball, Minnesota
Historical Society; p. 59—baking, Minnesota Historical Society; p. 63—FDR in car, Bettmann/CORBIS;
p. 65—REA poster, Rochester Institute of Technology; p. 69—Oriental treasures—© Sears, Roebuck
and Co., reprinted with permission; p. 73—Chinese Checkers, Library of Congress; p. 85—bananas,
© Danny Lehman/CORBIS; teacher's birthday, Minnesota Historical Society; p. 89—radio, printed
with permission of Emerson Radio Corp.; Clark Gable, Bettmann/CORBIS

Written by Jennifer Hirsch and Michelle Jones
Cover illustration by Walter Rane
Interior illustrations by Ann Boyajian and Walter Rane
Step-by-step illustrations by Susan McAliley and Geri Strigenz-Bourget
Photography by Kevin White and Jamie Young
Edited by Jennifer Hirsch
Designed and art directed by Lara Klipsch Elliott and Ingrid Slamer
Produced by Paula Moon and Richmond Powers
Historical research by Sally Wood

Library of Congress Cataloging-in-Publication Data

Kit's friendship fun.
p. cm.
Summary: Crafts, recipes, and games are designed to give a sense of the 1930s, or the period setting
for books in the American girls collection which features the character named Kit.
ISBN 1-58485-415-4
1. Handicraft—Juvenile literature. 2. Cookery, American—Juvenile literature. 3. United States—
Social life and customs—1918-1945—Juvenile literature. [1. Handicraft. 2. Cookery, American. 3.
United States—Social life and customs—1918-1945.]
TT171 .K48 2002
745.5—dc21   2001053815

**Special thanks to the children who tested
the crafts and recipes in this book and
gave us their valuable comments:**

Amy Albanese, Makenzie Amato, Meg Anderson,
Katelyn Austin, Katie Baldwin, Claire Burrington,
Samantha Bussan, Diana Camosy, Laura Checovich,
Nikki Close, Annie Cohen, Mei-Lien Converse, Jesse Daniel,
Chelsea Fine, Emily French, Rachel Gilbertson,
Hannah Green, Morgan Green, Shannon Green, Kari Hailey,
Rachel Hardy, Jessie Hausch, Danielle Hoffman,
Kendra Hutchins, Anna Jenewein, Caitlin Jenewein,
Madeleine Johnson, Kaela Kluever, Kelsey Kluever,
Lauren Kronser, Aubrey Lauersdorf, Grace Ledin,
Samantha Lindgren, Rachel Lokken, Alita Loper,
Marie Luebke, Kathryn McWilliams, Diane Mulnix,
Jessica Mulnix, Brianne Murray, Lauren Nelson,
Kelsey Peterson, Rachel Pientka, Kate Roth, Kristin Roth,
Dinah Rotter, Michelle Russell, Lauren Saad, Mary Scanlin,
Alyson Seeger, Rebecca Shulla, Brittany Smith, Kit Stanley,
Samantha Tolleson, Julia Wanke, Carolina Weakland-Warden,
Susannah Weakland-Warden, Katie Wipfli, Carmen Wood,
Kyle Wood, Nicole Wood, Madelyn Zaffino,
and Sarah Zander

THE BOOKS ABOUT KIT

MEET KIT • An American Girl
Kit Kittredge and her family get news that
turns their household upside down.

KIT LEARNS A LESSON • A School Story
It's Thanksgiving, and Kit learns a surprising
lesson about being thankful.

KIT'S SURPRISE • A Christmas Story
The Kittredges may lose their house.
Can Kit still find a way to make Christmas
merry and bright for her family?

HAPPY BIRTHDAY, KIT! • A Springtime Story
Kit loves Aunt Millie's thrifty ideas—until Aunt Millie
plans a pinch-penny party and invites Kit's whole class.

KIT SAVES THE DAY • A Summer Story
Kit's curiosity and longing for adventure
lead her to unexpected places—and into trouble!

CHANGES FOR KIT • A Winter Story
Kit writes a letter that brings changes and
new hope—in spite of the hard times.

◆

WELCOME TO KIT'S WORLD • 1934
American history is lavishly illustrated
with photographs, illustrations, and
excerpts from real girls' letters and diaries.